Sustainability Reporting for SMEs

Competitive Advantage through Transparency

T0331491

Elaine Cohen

Founder and CEO, Beyond Business Ltd

tw: @elainecohen

e: info@b-yond.biz

w: www.b-yond.biz

bl: www.csr-reporting.blogspot.com

bl: www.csrforhr.com

bl: www.csr-books.com

Author of *CSR for HR: A Necessary Partnership for Advancing Responsible Business Practices* (Greenleaf, 2010)

First published in 2013 by Dō Sustainability
87 Lonsdale Road, Oxford OX2 7ET, UK

ISBN 978-1-909293-37-3 (eBook-ePub)
ISBN 978-1-909293-38-0 (eBook-PDF)
ISBN 978-1-909293-36-6 (Paperback)

A catalogue record for this title is available from the British Library.

Dō Sustainability strives for net positive social and environmental impact. See our sustainability policy at **www.dosustainability.com**.

Page design and typesetting by Alison Rayner
Cover by Becky Chilcott

For further information on Dō Sustainability, visit our website:
www.dosustainability.com

DōShorts

Dō Sustainability is the publisher of **DōShorts**: short, high-value ebooks that distil sustainability best practice and business insights for busy, results-driven professionals. Each DōShort can be read in 90 minutes.

New and forthcoming DōShorts – stay up to date

We publish 3 to 5 new DōShorts each month. The best way to keep up to date? Sign up to our short, monthly newsletter. Go to **www.dosustainability.com/newsletter** to sign up to the Dō Newsletter. Some of our latest and forthcoming titles include:

- *Green Jujitsu: Embed Sustainability into Your Organisation* Gareth Kane
- *How to Make your Company a Recognised Sustainability Champion* Brendan May
- *Making the Most of Standards* Adrian Henriques
- *Promoting Sustainable Behaviour: A Practical Guide to What Works* Adam Corner
- *How to Account for Sustainability* Laura Musikanski
- *Sustainability in the Public Sector* Sonja Powell
- *Sustainable Transport Fuels Business Briefing* David Thorpe
- *The Changing Profile of Corporate Climate Change Risk* Mark Trexler & Laura Kosloff
- *The First 100 Days: Plan, Prioritise & Build a Sustainable Organisation* Anne Augustine
- *The Short Guide to Sustainable Investing* Cary Krosinsky
- *REDD+ and Business Sustainability* Brian McFarland

Subscriptions

In additional to individual sales and rentals, we offer individual and organisational subscriptions to our full collection of published and forthcoming books. To discuss a subscription for yourself or your organisation, email **veruschka@dosustainability.com**

Write for us, or suggest a DōShort

Please visit **www.dosustainability.com** for our full publishing programme. If you don't find what you need, write for us! Or suggest a DōShort on our website. We look forward to hearing from you.

....

Abstract

ELAINE COHEN OUTLINES THE PATH to sustainability transparency for small and medium-sized enterprises (SMEs). In this practical, easy to read e-book, Elaine looks at the unique role SMEs play in our economies, and provides guidance to SMEs on how to improve their competitive advantage and do better business through adopting not only a sustainable approach, but also a transparent approach. Reporting delivers much more than a printed word; it is a mechanism to help SMEs to develop, grow, communicate and gain greater trust with all stakeholders. This book is designed to help SMEs to align with global business expectations and to help managers in large corporations, who depend on an army of SMEs around the world, understand what they can and should demand from SME partners in their supply chain.

About the Author

 **ELAINE COHEN** is passionate about corporate social responsibility (CSR), human resources (HR), sustainability reporting, social justice and ice cream! Elaine is the founder and managing consultant of Beyond Business Ltd, an inspired CSR consulting and sustainability reporting firm, serving a long list of international companies. Prior to work in this field, Elaine gained over 20 years of business experience with Procter & Gamble (eight years in Supply Chain Executive roles in Europe), with Unilever (eight years as VP for Human Resources with Unilever Israel) and a range of other roles with smaller companies.

Elaine makes a contribution to the community as a Chair of a Women's Empowerment non-profit organisation and assisting students. Elaine lectures widely on CSR, is a committed blogger on sustainability reporting via her blog (www.csr-reporting.blogspot.com), provides Expert Reviews of Sustainability Reports for CorporateRegister.com (www.corporateregister. com) and *Ethical Corporation Magazine* (www.ethicalcorp.com) and writes in many printed journals and websites. Elaine authored the first ever book on the interface between CSR and HR (*CSR for HR*, Greenleaf, 2010).

Elaine holds a (double) Honours BA degree in Modern Languages from Bradford University, is Manchester (UK) born and has lived in Israel since 1990. She is married with two children.

Contents

Abstract 5

About the Author 7

Preface 13

Foreword 17

1   The SME Approach to CSR 21
   Defining SMEs 22
   Characteristics of SMEs 23
   CSR for SMEs 26
   The CSR–sustainability model 27

2   The State of Sustainability Reporting 31
   The current state of sustainability reporting 31
   Two main approaches to SME reporting 32
   CSR or Sustainability Report 32
   **GRI and the Sustainability
   Reporting Framework** 33
   The current state of SME reporting 34
   **The UN Global Compact Communication
   on Progress** 36

3   The Business Advantage of
    Transparency for SMEs.................................39
    Case Study 1: FPL 42
    Case Study 2: Impahla Clothing....................46
    Case Study 3: Banarra 52
    Perspectives from the three case studies 55

4   The Roadmap to Transparency
    for SMEs...57
    Mission..58
    Materiality 61
    Measure 64
    Manage 75
    Manifest...76

5   Guidance for Developing
    a Sustainability Report...............................77
    Sustainability Reports 77
    Ready!...81
    Steady!..83
    Go! 85
    Minimalist SME Sustainability Reports..............89

6   A Few More Words About Transparency.......91
    Your website 91
    Social media 91
    Multimedia options.................................92

Perfection 92

Gain competitive advantage 93

Links and Resources 95

Notes 99

Preface

THIS BOOK AIMS TO ENCOURAGE SMES to be more transparent in their business practices and leverage the power of sustainability reporting as a platform to develop increased competitiveness and long-term sustainable success. Yes, I believe that sustainability reporting helps companies to gain competitive advantage and even increase profits. This, of course, presupposes that sustainability reporting is part of a process of evolving sustainability practice in any company. Reporting is nothing if it is not founded in actual actions taken by a business to improve its sustainability impacts. The process of reporting, however, adds value which is much greater than the printed or online report itself. Reporting, done well, requires reflection, discussion and engagement and a willingness to voluntarily make public a set of promises that bind a company to its sustainability commitment. This is as true for SMEs as it is for any business anywhere. This book is an attempt to raise awareness and assist SMEs in developing the transparency habit so that they can become more competitive while contributing proactively to the sustainability of our society and planet.

I wanted to call this book 'Make More Money: Sustainability Reporting for SMEs', but one of the independent peer reviewers thought this was inappropriate. There is no point in having a book peer-reviewed if you are not going to listen to good advice. So I toned down the sensationalism, and modified the title. My original thought was the result of the influence of my brother, Philip Carlick, a retired (successful) SME business owner, who urges me to focus my sustainability conversations in a way which he believes is more meaningful to businesses. The cash value is what counts, he says. Don't just say we are working to create a better world. Say we will make more money. That's what SMEs understand, he tells me. So while I have my reservations about money being the most important thing for business, there is no doubt that many SMEs are often closer to the cash flow precipice (as I know from my own experience as an SME owner, and as my brother certainly experienced in over 30 years of business) than they would care to admit. Similarly, done right, sustainability practices leveraged through transparency, can lead to greater profits, as the case studies included in this book confirm.

For the purposes of this book, SMEs refer both to companies which meet the European Commission definition of medium-sized businesses (up to 250 employees and Euro 50 million in turnover) as well as to larger SMEs which may employ up to around 500 employees. Typically, these businesses represent the largest number of companies in any country, collectively engage the largest local workforce and contribute significantly to local economies. Many businesses of this size engage in some forms of Corporate Social Responsibility and Sustainability practices, sometimes reflecting the personal values of the founder/owner, sometimes in order to gain financial benefits and sometimes because they are encouraged to do so by their larger clients and customers. However, most businesses in this category do not invest in transparency about their sustainability practices. Similarly, sustainability practices in the SME world are generally intuitive and not formally structured, and outcomes are not measured, which makes it difficult to leverage such activity for competitive advantage.

This book asserts that those businesses which adopt a transparent approach, and report in one form or another on their sustainability practices, can gain significant business advantage, both in terms of more efficient and effective internal management processes and in terms of reputation and business-building. It also identifies the relevant tools available to assist SMEs in developing transparency, and provides guidance in how to get started.

This book is addressed primarily to SME business owners and/or managers, entrepreneurs, business students, business educators and small business consultants. In addition, sustainability managers in larger organisations may find this book helpful in assisting their organisations manage their supply chains which undoubtedly include several SMEs.

A personal note

I am both an SME owner and a CSR consultant and sustainability reporter. As an SME, we published our own first Sustainability Report in 2011, which can be viewed at our website: www.b-yond.biz/en/ sub_page.asp?sp=323&p=16. We were proud to win the CRRA '12 Best SME Report Award for this report, and also receive many positive comments and feedback from around the world from consultants, students, corporate practitioners and academics. We kept our report simple, short and focused on what we felt were relevant, material issues. We wrote the report ourselves and did not use external design, due to budget constraints. The value of reporting for us is threefold. *First*, demonstrating integrity. As sustainability reporters, it is unthinkable that we would not deliver our own report. *Second*, our report enabled us to showcase some of the great work our clients engaged us to help them progress, representing our gratitude for the opportunity to work with many fabulous companies and people. *Third*, our report is our expertise and, for a sustainability reporting firm, our best marketing tool. Writing the report caused us to reflect about our own strategy and practices, make some changes, seek explicit feedback from customers, and take the opportunity to go carbon neutral through the purchase of offsets. I believe our sustainability report has helped us to make more money, mainly through greater exposure for our business and expertise, and the acquisition of new clients from around the world. This book is a way of showing SMEs that it can be done, simply, effectively and without aiming for perfection.

Finally, I cannot write a book without dedicating it to my children, Eden and Amit Cohen, who love seeing their name in print! I am also grateful to Iris Rakovitzky who assisted in the research for this book.

Elaine Cohen
December 2012

Foreword

by Paul Scott
Managing Director, CorporateRegister.com Ltd

WHEN I HEARD that Elaine was working on a book about SME reporting I was delighted: SME reporting is vitally important, and I can't think of anyone better placed to uncover, analyse and address the issues.

Why is SME reporting so important?

All the headlines about CR (corporate responsibility) reporting are about large companies. Who reports, who doesn't, which sectors are fully engaged and which aren't, which companies report using reporting guidelines and assurance. . . the list goes on. At CorporateRegister. com we're guilty of the same mindset: we announce reports by leading companies, review reports, compile statistics. What we don't do is examine the totality of economic activity needing CR disclosure, benchmark the amount of activity being reported, and estimate the reporting gap. That is what needs to be done.

Why is there a reporting gap? Briefly, large companies are easy to track. Listed companies are the individual components of stock exchanges the world over, and it is these stock exchanges which give the daily indicators of economic activity, how well or badly a specific stock market is performing. To an extent, these companies act as a proxy for economic activity, in the same way as watching an iceberg drift shows the direction of wind and current – we can only see the part above the water line, but the entire iceberg moves as one unit. Stock exchanges track the 'visible' share prices for listed companies, and we assume these reflect the entire economy. However, those engaged in sustainability aren't interested in tracking a portfolio or index, they want to see the whole picture of business activity impacts across the planet.

To extend this analogy, in the same way that 50% to 99% of an iceberg's mass will be invisible, below the water line, the same proportion of the economy is accounted for by SMEs; at least that's the case in Europe (see http://ec.europa.eu/enterprise/policies/sme/index_en.htm) where the European Commission estimates that the region's 23 million SMEs account for 99% of the region's businesses, and contribute collectively to over half of the total value-added across the EU's 27 member states.

As a rule of thumb, 50% of CR happens in Europe – half the 45,000 reports profiled on CorporateRegister.com are European, half the reporting companies are European, half the 40,000 site users. It seems a fair assumption that the European Commission's statistics would hold true globally. However, CorporateRegister.com's statistics reveal that only around 4% of reporting companies all around the world are SMEs, so there is a yawning gulf between global economic activity and the number of companies publishing CR reports. We are making reporting headway amongst the world's largest companies, but we have barely begun amongst the world's SMEs.

Why is this so? Well, only in a few countries are aspects of CR reporting starting to become mandatory, and then only for large companies. SMEs just don't have the resources, the incentives or the knowledge to report, especially given that (again, taking European Commission data) nine out of ten SMEs are in fact micro-companies with fewer than ten employees. It is unlikely that any country will introduce any form of mandatory reporting for SMEs, so what these enterprises choose to disclose will remain entirely voluntary far into the foreseeable future. At the same time the expectations underlying CR reporting are becoming more onerous, even for large multinationals. Materiality assessments, frameworks, stakeholder evaluations, independent assurance – as the CR reporting bar is raised progressively higher, soon it will be so high that only very well-resourced companies clear it. How can we expect SMEs to address CR reporting?

Simple online tools must be one route. Inventive financial incentives, perhaps coupled with preferential supply chain treatment may be another. Elaine has many insights in this field.

Elaine Cohen leads her very own SME and has many SME clients. As a global authority in the CR field she is exceptionally well versed in the pros and cons, do's and don'ts of CR reporting for all sizes of company, which is why her insights into SME reporting are so valuable.

I'd like to make a prediction. I predict that in ten years we will look back and wonder how those engaged in CR and sustainability could so long have been blind to the importance of SMEs. Those of us with a copy of this book will recognise that at least one person had the required foresight – so thank you Elaine.

Paul Scott is director of CorporateRegister.com Ltd, the world's most comprehensive directory of CR reports, with an archive stretching back to 1990 and profiling over 45,000 reports.

. . . .

CHAPTER 1

The SME Approach to CSR

IN THIS CHAPTER, WE WILL:

- Define what we mean by SME

- Provide a perspective of the role of SMEs in our national and global economies

- Explore the characteristics of SMEs and the way they differ from MNEs

- Introduce the concept of CSR and a roadmap to sustainable business

SMEs are often regarded as the powerhouse of our global economy because they employ most of the world's employees and generate close to half our global economic output. Many SMEs form an essential part of the extended supply chain of larger national and multinational companies, who rely on the products, services and focused expertise of these smaller companies to help them achieve growth. In fact, many global companies have a business model which is entirely dependent upon SMEs in their supply chain, such as Nike, who reports having 600 factories employing over 820,000 people in 46 countries involved in the manufacture of Nike products.[1]

SME development and growth is an economic priority for many regions in the world. In Europe, SMEs remain 'the backbone of the European economy, with some 20.7 million firms accounting for more than 98 per cent of all enterprises'. These SMEs employ 67% of Europe's total 87 million workers, and deliver 58% of gross value added.[2] In the Europe 2020 strategy, where a top priority is increasing employment opportunities and raising the employment rate, while reducing poverty and social exclusion, support for SMEs and the entrepreneurship which is often associated with small business creativity and agility, is a central theme.[3] In the Asia-Pacific region, where SMEs form 90% of total companies and 60% of the workforce, SMEs have been noted as a 'key to building state of the art economies' and support is targeted at removing barriers to trade and encouraging start-ups.[4] In China alone, there are 42 million small- and medium-sized businesses. In the US, the latest 2007 Census recorded close to six million SMEs with a total of over 60 million employees and sales revenue of over $11 billion.[5] SMEs are the largest group of US exporters and the largest users of imported goods. A focus of US government policy is to assist SMEs to grow their exports.

Defining SMEs:
500 employees/Euro 50 million turnover

The level of SME activity differs considerably in markets around the globe, as indeed does the definition of what an SME constitutes. The European Commission definition of an SME[6] covers medium-sized businesses which employ below 250 people and generate revenues of below Euro 50 million, and micro-business, which employ below 10 people and generate revenues of below Euro 2 million. In the US, however, SMEs tend to include all companies of below 500 people and revenues reaching below approximately $25 million.[7] In China, there exists a complex matrix of definitions which differentiates by sector and business type, and includes businesses which employ up to 2000 people with revenues of over $190 million[8] at the upper limit. For the purposes of this book, we will apply an upper limit of approximately 500 employees and Euro 50 million or USD 65 million in revenue. This keeps us in the range of companies which have largely similar characteristics, mainly local (though they may sell products or services internationally) and often privately owned.

Having said this, the SME sector is three sectors all in one, encompassing micro-businesses with up to 10 employees, smaller businesses with up to 50 or so employees and all the rest. These types of businesses are inherently different. A company with up to ten people may always feel like a start-up, whereas a company with 500 people needs structure, processes, frameworks and a very strong communications programme. In terms of CSR, however, opportunities abound for all types of SMEs and, as we shall see, are available to be tailored to meet the specific company profile, structure and state of mind of any business in the SME category.

Characteristics of SMEs

Given the diversity of SMEs, it is difficult to generalise, but we can discern 12 key characteristics that typify most of the companies in this category (see Figure 1). Probably the most significant feature here is the very dominant presence in most SMEs of the owner-founder who remains at the helm of the company throughout its life, which may include the subsequent handing of leadership to family members who have grown up with the business. While many exceptions exist, in which small companies have grown into larger corporations, the vast majority of

SMEs remain SMEs throughout their lifetime and continue to be guided by their founding spirit. Often, given the nature of entrepreneurs, smaller business owners drive their business from a sense of passion to see a change in the world or provide a service which they deeply believe offers value to society, often based on what they are personally able to achieve or accomplish because of the skills and experience they have acquired. This aspect of SMEs – the initial values-based passion for change and contribution to society – which often transcends an absolute desire to put profit at the top of the priority list, is what typically draws SMEs closer

FIGURE 1. Key characteristics of SMEs

✓ VALUES: Built on founder-manager values, skills and initiatives.

✓ CONTROL: Private, independent and autonomous.

✓ STRUCTURE: Simple structure, fast, agile, flexible decision-making.

✓ PLANNING: Unstructured planning and budgeting processes.

✓ MARKETS AND RELATIONSHIPS: Personal relationships, local networks, predominantly local markets

✓ FINANCE: Low overheads, but limited access to finance.

✓ CULTURE: Direct, informal, personal culture. Entrepreneurial spirit.

✓ PEOPLE: Local people, multi-skilled, multi-taskers, flexible and engaged.

✓ RESOURCES: Limited resources and limited scope.

✓ DEPENDENCE: High dependence on market conditions and clients.

✓ COMMUNITY: Locally oriented and connected.

✓ SOCIAL MEDIA: Early adopter of Social Media tools.

to one of the fundamental tenets of a CSR approach: values-based, ethical, humanely driven business which has a clear understanding of its role in society. (Of course, many SME founders are motivated primarily by the need to earn a living but even so, they often remain true to a set of core values.)

Other key characteristics of SMEs which help these companies survive and thrive include a lack of formal (and bureaucratic) structure, creativity and ability to develop highly focused expertise which is relevant to local and global value chains. Driven by a vision for change, SMEs recognise opportunities as they arise, often intuitively, and are able to make changes to adapt and exploit such opportunities with a quick response and a practical ability for creative improvisation. Often part of a local community, SMEs maintain close ties with their local networks and surround themselves with relationships which are based on trust throughout the long term, providing a buffer against potential risk or unforeseen adversity. Additionally, SMEs have largely become early adopters of the incredible range of tools available on social media, which are largely cost-free and enable small businesses to achieve a presence on the internet through blogs, Twitter, Facebook, LinkedIn, YouTube and many others. SMEs who have something to say now have a range of channels they can exploit to make their voice heard, gain recognition and become a part of a national or even global business network. More importantly, strong use of these tools brings new business. I recall the time I heard Twitter founder Biz Stone talk about how a local bakery would use Twitter to inform customers that a new batch of freshly baked loaves were just about to go on sale. The loaves were snapped up before he could get the last one out of the oven. As an SME founder-owner myself, I can categorically say that the vast majority of business that we do is a direct result of our strong internet presence. This is true for business in our local market, and absolutely true for global business which now exceeds 50% of our revenue.

On the other hand, these fantastic advantages of SMEs, which larger corporations often envy, have their corresponding downside. Owner-dependence may lead to lack of ability to grow beyond an initial, possibly limited, vision. Intuitive decision-making may lack the broad consultation necessary to reach balanced or better outcomes. Lack of structure, planning and evaluation of risk may dictate an inability to leverage resources to increase scale and go beyond current boundaries. Lack of financial planning may result in cash-flow problems strangulating the business, especially as access to financing is often elusive or expensive. Social media presence may take up much time, but may not be targeted in a way which delivers best responses.

CSR for SMEs

As a concept, CSR is a way of doing business and not an addition to doing business. Sustainability at its core should assist companies in doing better business both in the short term and the long term. Many SMEs are already doing this, even though they might not call it CSR, or sustainability, by virtue of the values that drive their business, the personal relationships they maintain with employees and customers (stakeholder engagement) and the desire to make a contribution to society. SMEs can leverage the advantages of CSR, building on this inherent alignment with sustainability principles, through adopting a more structured and transparent approach.

While a full-blown sustainability programme which has global impact, such as the approach of Unilever, in the Sustainable Living Plan,[9] or Kingfisher, the home improvement retailer, which has declared a 'net positive' approach to doing business,[10] or of Nestlé, which has pioneered the 'shared value' business model,[11] may seem beyond the reach of the SME community of businesses, SMEs must remember that somewhere they are part of the global value chain. Somewhere, an MNE[12] is relying upon an army of SMEs to support its own business sustainability. Somewhere, a consumer is affected by the actions of several SMEs. Everywhere, SME employees deserve the same protection of their rights as MNE employees; SME customers deserve the same opportunity to have their aspirations and concerns addressed; SME suppliers, often SMEs themselves, must be brought on board with the collective effort. Not being big is not a reason, and certainly not an excuse, not to embrace the principles and practices of a sustainable business. By making CSR part of the way they do business SMEs gain business benefit while making a respectable and necessary contribution to our ability to live well, now and in the future, and protect our planet.

The CSR–sustainability model

I often work with a simple model which shows the process of sustainability in action in companies. While typically I use this framework with larger companies, it can be applied to smaller businesses.

The concept is simple: CSR (or sustainability, which we use as inter-changeable terms), lies within a tunnel of three prerequisites:

1. **Leadership and strategy:** these are necessary to provide the drive, support, authority and long-term thinking necessary for a successful CSR-aligned business model.

2. **Ethics:** an ethical approach to doing business is not CSR. It is a necessary prerequisite of CSR.

3. **Governance:** a clear direction from the Board of Directors, or in the case of SMEs, the company management, who ensure the right controls, risk management processes and compliance frameworks are in place.

Once these prerequisites are in place, to a greater or lesser degree, the process of developing a sustainable business and sustainable contribution to society can move forward with consistency and purpose. For larger corporations, this makes sense. For SMEs, leadership, ethics and governance may be more implicit rather than explicit. A good exercise for any SME would be to try to articulate these prerequisites more specifically: a statement of vision and mission, a set of values and brief

Code of Ethics, a statement of the company's management approach or key policies and procedures for key company processes together with an analysis of the risks and challenges the company faces, and pathways to overcome the risks. These are not difficult things to do; but they require a few hours away from the daily routine to think, discuss and formulate. The process may well deliver some insights about the SME business and how to progress along the sustainability journey.

Once the prerequisites are in place, we categorise the sustainability roadmap progression into five stages, which are not necessarily a linear progression, but more of an interactive and iterative process, where companies may start at the beginning, end or middle and move back and forth as their processes, understanding and experiences evolve.

- ✓ **Materiality:** this is the identification of the most important (material) issues from a sustainability standpoint that any business should address, and requires consultation with key stakeholders in order to achieve a full and considered conclusion.

- ✓ **Responsibility:** this is the different actions your company takes to minimise the negative impacts of the different types of your business activity on people, society and the planet. This is sometimes referred to as 'do no harm'.

- ✓ **Shared value:** this is the opportunity area of sustainability. It relates to creating a social benefit through innovative new business solutions thereby generating economic and social benefits.

- ✓ **Transparency:** this is about reflecting your sustainability performance in a balanced, comprehensive and accurate way, to your stakeholders, so that they can make informed decisions about their relationship with your business.

✓ **Sustainability:** this is not really a phase, it is the outcome of all the prior phases. However, it is almost never a destination, but a journey. Achieving 100% sustainability is not possible by one business as all businesses are interdependent to some degree, and part of the grand global ecosphere. In this phase, as a business, you are maturing into consideration of the wider global issues that affect our society and planet, and joining or forming partnerships to drive more systemic sustainable solutions.

These five phases are cyclical and never-ending. As a business matures into the final phase, it should loop back to reassessing materiality and realign the roadmap for continuous improvement.

As SMEs, you have a part to play in every one of the phases in the CSR Roadmap, and each phase contributes to your ability to gain competitive advantage over the short, medium and long term.

....

CHAPTER 2

The State of Sustainability Reporting

IN THIS CHAPTER, WE WILL:

- Briefly review the state of sustainability reporting and introduce the Global Reporting Initiative

- Examine the state of SME reporting and transparency

- Explore the current trends that are driving even greater transparency from SMEs

The current state of sustainability reporting

SUSTAINABILITY REPORTING TODAY is largely regarded as approaching mainstream. The 2011 international survey of corporate responsibility reporting by the large accounting firm KPMG[13] confirms that '95% of the largest 250 companies in the world publish Corporate Responsibility Reports' and describes CSR reporting as having 'come of age' and as the 'new de facto law' for companies. This is reinforced by the fact that in some countries, corporate responsibility reporting has become a regulatory requirement. Also, the fact that the number of sustainability reports published each year since 1992 has continued to grow, reaching an estimated 8000+ in 2012, if you include the many local language reports that are not currently on the radars of most lists. However, this being said, reporting is still very much the territory of the larger corporations, especially multinationals. Of the tens of thousands of transnational companies all around the world, only a handful has made sustainability reporting a way of life. Only a very minute percentage of SMEs disclose sustainability information in some way.

Two main approaches to SME reporting

SMEs publicly report on corporate responsibility broadly in two ways, in addition to less formal approaches to communicating CSR or sustainability messages on company websites. These are:

1. CSR or Sustainability Report

2. UN Global Compact Communication on Progress

CSR or Sustainability Report

We define the Sustainability Report as a comprehensive and balanced account of a company's material sustainability (economic, environmental and social) impacts, and general sustainability performance, covering a specific time frame, in one place. The Sustainability Report may come in different shapes, sizes and formats, including print or wholly online versions. One SME, MHPM Project Managers Inc., recently published its report as a creative infographic![14] The key is that the report must refer to a specific time period (usually one or two years) and that all the information is available and identifiable as relating to that time frame. For the purposes of this book, and often in general, the Sustainability Report refers to what we might also term the CR Report, CSR Report or even Corporate Accountability or Corporate Citizenship report.

GRI and the Sustainability Reporting Framework[15]

At this point, it seems appropriate to introduce the Global Reporting Initiative (GRI), a pivotal influence in any discussion about sustainability reporting. GRI was established in 2001 as a multi-stakeholder, network-based organisation, headquartered in Amsterdam, the Netherlands, and now boasts more than 600 core supporters and some 30,000 people representing different sectors and constituencies.

GRI has pioneered and developed a comprehensive Sustainability Reporting Framework that is widely used around the world. The Framework provides guidance for organisations to measure and report their economic, environmental, social and governance performance. Specifically, the recommended content includes: information about the company and its approach to sustainability management (Profile Disclosures); its core policies, procedures, processes (Management Approach Disclosures), and a set of qualitative and quantitative performance disclosures covering different aspects of sustainability impacts (Performance Indicators). An essential part of the Reporting Framework is the detailed guidance on methodology for reporting against different indicators, designed, in theory at least, to enable some form of comparability between the voluntary disclosures of different companies. In practice, this comparability has been hard to achieve, partly because of the way the Framework is used by companies and partly because of some ambiguities inherent in the Framework itself. The GRI Framework is now undergoing revision (it has already been revised in the past) and the new version (called 'G4')[27] is scheduled for launch in May 2013.

The current GRI Reporting Framework provides companies with an option to select a level of transparency which they find appropriate for their business and its stage on the sustainability journey. There are three levels:

- ✓ **Application Level A:** the most transparent option, requiring disclosures against all the Profile and Management disclosures and all core Performance Indicators in the Framework.

- ✓ **Application Level B:** a comprehensive (and the most popular) option, requiring disclosures against Profile and Management disclosures and 20 Performance Indicators in the Framework.

- ✓ **Application Level C:** a lower transparency option, suitable for smaller businesses or first-time reporting companies, requiring Profile disclosures and ten Performance Indicators in the Framework.

Companies may declare their Reporting Level using the Framework guidance provided by the GRI, thereby giving stakeholders an upfront expectation of what transparency level to expect.

As the only comprehensive reporting framework available today, the GRI Framework has become the perceived best-practice standard for sustainability reporting.

The current state of SME reporting

The most reliable source of information about published CSR or Sustainability Reports is CorporateRegister.com,[16] and its Managing Director, Paul Scott, to whom I am grateful for statistics about SME reporting presented in this chapter. While there are inevitably some reports that do not get on the radar, I have found over the years that CorporateRegister.com is an excellent reflection of how reporting is evolving and where the trends can be found.

. . . .

FIGURE 2. SME sustainability reporting through the years

© CorporateRegister.com Ltd 2012

. . . .

In 2011, the CorpororateRegister.com database shows that 293 SME CSR reports were published in 2011, a figure which has increased every single year since the start of the database almost 20 years ago (see Figure 2). The years 2006–2009 represented a high-growth period for SME reporting, moving from only 79 reports in 2005 to 286 reports in 2010, adding 30–40 reports per year. This slowed in 2011, with only seven more SME reports published than in 2010, and in 2012, for which full-year data are not available at the time of writing – the total figure looks as though it will not exceed that of 2011 by much, if at all. SME report publication included an average of 50 first-time reporters per year in these peak reporting years.

Following a similar trend in large company reporting, the vast majority of early SME reports until about 2002 were focused on environmental reporting. Since then, SMEs have matured with over 90% of reports

FIGURE 3. Top ten countries for SME reporting

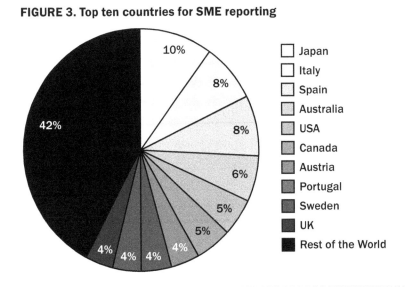

providing a fuller view of company performance and impacts as Corporate Responsibility or Sustainability Reports. And if you are wondering which countries are the strongest in SME reporting, see Figure 3. Japan, Italy, Spain, Australia and the US lead the pack.

Around half of the SME reports published in recent years follow the GRI Reporting Framework and between 20 and 25% are externally verified.[17]

The UN Global Compact Communication on Progress

Another type of reporting preferred by many SMEs is the UN Global Compact Communication on Progress (COP). While not usually referred to as a 'Sustainability Report' as the Communication on Progress is structured around ten basic principles of responsible business, rather than the more holistic scope of sustainability reporting, the COP offers a lightweight solution for companies wanting to develop transparency without the intensive detail that a GRI report requires. The UN Global Compact (UNGC) is the largest global CSR initiative and counts over 7000 business participants. Participation requires two things: a written declaration by the head of the company to uphold the ten principles of the Global Compact, and an annual communication (COP) on how the company is upholding its commitment. Companies which fail to publish a COP are expelled by the UNGC. The advantage of the UNGC COP is that it enables companies to focus on the good work they are doing in sustainability terms, without the rigorous requirement of a set of specific performance indicators.

In recent years, the UNGC has made some structural changes which increase alignment of UNGC COP disclosures with the GRI Reporting framework. There is now a tiered approach in which the highest level COP is comparable to the GRI framework at Application Level A. However, at the more basic (active) level, the COP is a much easier entry level for SMEs who want to start reporting.

In 2011, SMEs (up to 250 employees) made up 54% of the total UNGC company base. Spain, France, Japan, Brazil and US have the highest representation of SMEs which participate in the UNGC, with Spain being highly popular (600 of the total 900 Spanish UNGC participants), supported, apparently, by a focused initiative to encourage responsible practice by SMEs in Spain and support their development within the framework of adherence to the ten principles.[18]

One of the biggest challenges of the UNGC is the relatively low level of SME compliance with reporting requirements. SMEs display a much

. . . .

FIGURE 4. Active UNGC SMEs (2010)[20]

Status of participants in Global Compact more than 2 years

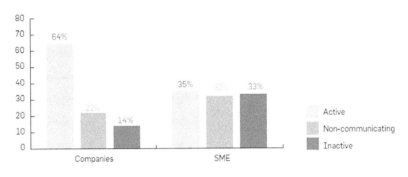

lower reporting rate than large companies (whose full Sustainability Report often serves as both a report and a COP).

SMEs represent 68% of all expelled companies which totalled 3011 by end of 2011 and the UNGC writes in its 10 year Anniversary Annual Review in 2009 that SMEs 'consistently face difficulty maintaining an "active" status'.[19] For UNGC participants who have been engaged for more than two years, 35% of SMEs tend to maintain active status with an annual COP whereas 64% of larger companies are able to do so.

Despite good intentions, SMEs find it very difficult to achieve a consistent level of annual reporting on sustainability, whether via the full report or the COP route.

In this book, we will not discuss in detail the process for writing COPs but will focus on Sustainability Reports. We will also try to demonstrate that reporting for SMEs is a worthwhile investment.

. . . .

CHAPTER 3

The Business Advantage of Transparency for SMEs

IN THIS CHAPTER, WE WILL:

- Reconfirm the business advantages of SME reporting

- Hear from some SME business leaders who confirm that transparency is better business

SMEs are close to their founders, who often remain as founder-managers throughout the lifetime of the SME. Some SMEs transition well from micro- to small- to medium-sized businesses and eventually manage to become large corporations. Others remain, many by design, small, specialist, niche businesses, driven by – and often limited by – the capabilities of the founder. Whatever the size an SME plateaus at, the very fact that it survives means that it is playing an important role in the value chain of some other business, somewhere, either upstream or downstream. It is this fact which is the most compelling case for SMEs to report, and is exemplified in the case study about Impahla Clothing which you can read later in this chapter.

The key business benefits for SME reporting are not dissimilar to those reported by big companies. Generating trust through transparency which leads to customer appreciation and increased sales, engaged employees, improved access to finance, improved relationships with local communities, improved internal processes and structures for managing risk are all examples of how companies gain benefit from a sustainability approach. These reporting benefits apply equally to small and large businesses. Specific examples of these benefits are illustrated in three 'Case in Point' stories later in this chapter.

There is one target audience for sustainability reporting which is primarily the focus of large companies and far less of smaller companies: the investment community, including private and institutional investors, investment houses and investment analysts. Typically, SMEs are privately owned, have far fewer legal disclosure obligations and are not subject to scrutiny by the investment community, which has in recent years started to wake up to the potential of non-financial risks to impact the financial performance of a business over time. Happily, most SMEs fly under the radar. However, SMEs often need financing in order to grow, and turn to banks to secure loans. A robust sustainability disclosure will often make a significant positive impact on potential lenders, and may even lead to preferential interest rates.

However, as mentioned above, as the interest in the sustainability performance of large companies grows, so will the interest in how these large companies manage their supply chains. Here again, SMEs will find themselves having to operate in a sustainable manner and disclose key performance data required by large companies for their own reporting.

Even without investor interest, other SME stakeholder groups can significantly impact on the potential to survive and thrive. Customers, employees, local community networks and others can all play a role in affecting the business performance of an SME. By adopting a sustainability approach, SMEs can ensure they are ahead of the game and keep adapting their business to the evolving needs of all their stakeholders.

I confess that, as a small business, providing services to large companies around the world, we have been lazy about reviewing the quality of our customer service. The work we do typically requires us to maintain a close relationship with customers over prolonged periods of time, during which we work together closely as partners in joint projects with shared objectives. Generally, we 'feel' that things are going well, and usually, we get some (positive!) feedback on the outcome of our work. However, we have not developed the habit of formally requesting feedback on our performance as a supplier. We conducted a formal customer survey for the first time in preparation for our first Sustainability Report in early 2011, and the responses were very positive, though some comments caused us to rethink whether we are working in the most effective way. It was valuable to receive this feedback. (We used an anonymous free online survey tool.[21]) As we are now approaching the time to write our second Sustainability Report, I realised that not only must we do this again, but that, in fact, we should develop a mechanism to gain formal feedback more quickly throughout the year. Therefore, in addition to our online survey, we will develop a feedback process which enables customers to rate all aspects of our service immediately upon conclusion of every project. This may seem like a simple thing, and something we advise our clients to do all the time, but as soon as we thought of doing this ourselves it felt so appropriate that we wondered why we hadn't done it before. I am sure this will help us improve our service and our relationships with our clients. The point is that the reporting process was the catalyst for this change. If we had not promised ourselves to report transparently on our performance, we would almost certainly not have thought about this customer engagement process.

The benefits of reporting are clear in theory. Now, let's hear from three companies who can confirm they are clear in practice.

Case Study 1: FPL

FORENSIC PATHWAYS LTD (FPL) (www.forensic-pathways.com) is an award-winning company with offices in the UK and Australia, and an international distributor network. FPL offers unique data analysis solutions in the area of mobile phone forensics, criminal intelligence, due diligence, risk and business intelligence and is internationally recognised for taking a lead in the development of forensic products and services. Founded in 2001, FPL benefits from a visionary founder, Deb Leary, who is an entrepreneur and recognised business leader holding a number of roles which serve the common good, such as the National President of the British Association of Women Entrepreneurs (www.bawe-uk.org), Deputy Director of the United Nations UK Global Compact Network (www. ungc-uk.net) and more. In recognition for her commitment to entrepreneurship Deborah was awarded an OBE in the Queen's Birthday Honours List in 2008 and was named British Female Inventor of the Year in 2005, just two in a string of awards she has received. It is not surprising then, that a visionary entrepreneur with a deep sense of values should establish a business which demonstrates strong social values.

In 2005, FPL signed on as a participant in the UN Global Compact, and has delivered an annual Communication on Progress since 2007.

Practitioner Insight

DEB LEARY OBE, FRSA

CEO Forensic Pathways Ltd

Why did you decide to participate in the UN Global Compact?

I hadn't really taken a lot of notice about CSR, I didn't think it applied to us as a small business. We were behaving that way anyway – ethical practices, integrity – I didn't realise there was more we could be doing. When I heard of the UN Global Compact, it made perfect sense for me. It is prescriptive, but it also recognises the human challenges of doing business and continuing to evolve. I thought this would give us an opportunity to challenge ourselves to improve further, and even to gain some recognition for the work we are doing. When I went to my first network event, someone asked me: 'How many people are there in your CSR Department?' I said: 'You are looking at her!'

What value did you see in producing an annual Communication on Progress?

As we continued to be a part of the Global Compact network, we thought about how we would develop our communications. Reporting became an extension of what we were doing anyway. It forces us to look at all aspects of what we are doing and ensure we manage it. We have found that reporting informs our business planning process – it becomes part of the business plan and not something separate from that. Reporting is not about who has got the best report and the glossiest magazine. The real question is how connected people are to that report. Proper reporting is about stripping CSR right back to what it is about – fundamental good business practice.

What have been the tangible benefits of reporting for FPL as an SME?

SMEs are an essential part of business – we have a skill base that we can bring to larger corporations. We must work in partnership and collaboration – if you don't work together, you are a fool. Most of the collaborative work we have done with corporations has been made much easier by the fact that we produce our annual report for the Global Compact. They know who we are, it attracts more interest in us as a company. It's a pleasure to be able to fill in the New Vendor forms from customers and know that our information is available in one place without having to scramble around for policy documents at the last minute. Also, the quality of the clients we get these days is a testimony to the value of our transparency. It shows we are a company looking beyond our current status, aspiring to be better. It inspires trust. The most important word in our business is integrity. This is true also for other stakeholders – all our employees see the report, of course, and we send it to our vast network of distributors, and this helps increase trust.

Is reporting a major burden for you as an SME?

Reporting is like everything else, you have to plan your resources. Sometimes we have been backed up and the report has been completed at the eleventh hour, but in general, we plan it in. We don't wait until the end of the year to think about it, either. We have a CSR file that we maintain throughout the year and whenever there is anything relevant to our CSR activities, we add it in, so that when the reporting time comes, we have a core of relevant material. We produce our report in-house, by ourselves. We also don't expect to be perfect. We do the best we can with the resources we have. That's far better than doing nothing, in my eyes.

Are your employees involved in preparing the report?

Yes. As the report is part of our business planning process, our team is naturally involved in what we do in the CSR area, and therefore what gets reported. Employees review the report before we publish it.

Top tips for SME reporters?

1. It's in the planning – it doesn't need to be onerous – it should be part of what you do.

2. Collect your material throughout the year – don't leave it to the last minute.

3. You don't need to be perfect – something is better than nothing.

Case Study 2: Impahla Clothing

SPRING ROMANCE PROPERTIES 34 (PTY) LIMITED, trading as Impahla Clothing (www.impahla.co.za) is a privately owned manufacturing company of world-class sport and lifestyle apparel and fabric. Based in Cape Town, South Africa, Impahla Clothing manufactures garments under a sole source agreement for PUMA and a newly acquired fabrics division manufactures premium knit fabrics. Impahla strives to achieve the highest standards as a supplier of quality fabrics, garment manufacturing and branding services. Impahla started trading in 2004, after the current Managing Director and largest shareholder, William Hughes, had bought the assets of an ailing garment business and realised that a new approach was demanded if this business were to succeed in the highly competitive garment market. Today, Impahla has grown from a business employing 60 people in 2004 to 234 in 2012, and generates revenues of R38 million (around 3.3 million Euros).

Impahla started reporting on sustainability performance with a first GRI Application Level C+ Sustainability Report for 2007 and has consistently delivered a Sustainability Report each year since then. For the first time, in 2012 Impahla published an Integrated Report in line with the recommendations of the Report on Governance for South Africa (King III), and conforming to GRI Application Level A. All Impahla's reports are available on the company website: www.impahla.co.za/Sustainability.html

Practitioner Insight

William Hughes
Shareowner and Managing Director,
Impahla Clothing

What made you start your sustainability reporting journey?

We know that the clothing industry in South Africa was in serious decline and that we would have to have a total change of thinking, be different from all the rest so that customers would actually want to come to us. There was no way we could import from the Far East. This pressure led us to focus on two things: being close to our people – you can't do anything if your people aren't with you – and truly understanding our customers. PUMA became a high priority account for Impahla and we appreciated their leadership in sustainability practices. When we were invited to take part in a reporting project with PUMA and the GRI, we were delighted. We didn't see this as a threat or a burden. On the contrary, we saw it as an opportunity to formalise what we were actually doing, so others could learn about us. We never hid anything, and remain very open, so reporting was a natural extension of our business practice.

How do you manage to assign the resources for reporting?

We do not have massive resources, and every cost however small in our business has to be justified, but we see clear advantages of being transparent, and not only because this is encouraged by our now sole customer, PUMA. Our relationship with PUMA is crucial and benefits from complete transparency about our business practices and our production programming. Our business philosophy is aligned with theirs, and underscored by the lengthy process we went through in formalising our understanding of corporate responsibility as one of PUMA's strategic suppliers. We believe our alignment to PUMA's business philosophy is an important factor that will ensure the sustainability of our supplier status with the company. We have continued to report in a sustainable manner, using external resources that can assist us at a reasonable price level. It is getting more expensive as we grow, but we believe this is important and make the resources available without this becoming a financial burden.

Impahla is privately owned SME, employing fewer than 250 employees and serving only one customer. What's the justification for publishing Sustainability Reports?

PUMA is not our only stakeholder, even if they are our only customer. They were delighted with our Integrated Report for 2011 and were amazed that we published our financials. However, we deal with other organisations: banks, suppliers, other funding organisations and local municipalities. Our report tells them everything they need to know about us as a company. Everybody wants to know about you these days. It's easier to do business and even more cost-effective. For example, we are able to secure funding for upgrading our plant at interest levels way below prime. Financial services providers see our sustainable approach and give Impahla a very positive credit rating.

What are the true benefits of reporting for Impahla?

I think that a lot of people focus on the wrong things. Greed is one of the worst factors that come into small business: therefore the businesses become unsustainable. A sustainability approach focuses you on the bigger picture – we want to be here in 20 years' time. It's not about how much you can put in your pocket now. While sustainability is more about what you do, and not just about reporting, the benefits of reporting are very clear.

First, it's about staff. If your staff is not on your side, that's a risk. For example, in 2009, there was an industry strike for three weeks. Not one of our staff went on strike – they are all members of the union. Our absenteeism level is 1.4% compared to 6–8% in local industry. Our policies have empowered our staff. We promote from within and our middle management is all home-grown. Employees stay with our business. This is both cost-efficient in human resources terms and supports business continuity.

Second, our relationship with PUMA. Our revenues have grown 633% since 2005. This is a direct outcome of the sustainable policies we have put into place which are made clear through our transparent reporting. It is not by chance that PUMA made us a strategic partner.

Third, the environment. We looked clearly at our issues and saw that electricity is the biggest contributor to our carbon footprint. We looked for ways to reduce our emissions and also operate more cost-efficiently. We installed an array of solar panels which now generate 25% of our requirement, giving us both cost savings and enabling us to become a carbon neutral manufacturer. We also planted over 2300 trees in local areas. These are fruit trees so that there is a benefit to local communities, and this enhances our reputation while improving our environment.

Top tips for SME reporters?

1. You need to do it. It is a benefit for your business. It also helps others.

2. Be honest and open. It builds trust.

3. Assign the right resources, modestly, without letting reporting become a financial burden.

Case Study 3: Banarra

BANARRA PTY LTD (www.banarra.com) is an active contributor to the sustainability landscape, both in Australia and globally, through a range of consultancy activities offering specialised support to organisations in the business, government and not-for-profit sectors looking to develop or enhance their sustainability approach, performance and accountability. Banarra's service lines are: Social and Human Rights; Strategy and Transformation; Accountability (including assurance and reporting), and Environment and Climate Change. Operating from offices in New South Wales, Australia, Banarra has a staff of 14 people and revenues of just over two million Australian dollars (approximately 1.6 million Euros).

Banarra is one of the few sustainability consulting SMEs around the world that publish sustainability reports and this is all the more remarkable when you consider that Banarra has published an annual sustainability report since 2006, the most recent report for 2011 being the company's sixth. All reports have followed the GRI Reporting Framework with the first at Application Level C and the most recent at Application Level B. Reports can be viewed on Banarra's website: www.banarra.com/about-us/our-reporting

The company name, Banarra, is an aboriginal word of Larrakia origin meaning 'ear'. This is because, according to Banarra, 'listening is a critical skill for a sustainability practitioner'.

Practitioner Insight

RICHARD BOELE
Founder and Managing Director,
Banarra Pty Ltd

What drove you to start reporting on Banarra's sustainability performance?

We conducted a customer satisfaction survey in 2005, and this formed the basis of our first report. We felt that the best way to build our relationship with clients was to put the results of client satisfaction in the public domain. We did this consistently for five years, with customer satisfaction being a significant section of the report, and then we moved to full sustainability reporting. We see this as 'walk the talk', demonstrating integrity. We provide advice on sustainability – surely we can demonstrate that we can do that ourselves?

What have been the challenges of sustainability reporting for an SME such as Banarra?

We knew that we had to produce a good quality report. Because of the nature of our business, we have to do it properly. At first, it felt like the 'nice-to-have' project and wasn't treated with the same degree of professionalism as the work we do for clients. Now, we have established a system to handle internal projects including our sustainability report in exactly the same way as we would plan and execute a reporting assignment for a client. This was a challenge at first, but now it is a significant benefit.

What have been the other benefits of sustainability reporting for Banarra?

It's not always easy to quantify the tangible benefits. However, we have won trophies for our reporting, including ACCA awards in Australia three times and awards in the CRRA online reporting awards for best first-time report and more. This recognition helps to ensure that employees are motivated and understand the wider context of what we do and our impacts. When we started reporting, we saw it predominantly as a client driver, to help us build trust with our existing clients and gain new clients. Now, we see reporting primarily as a mechanism for engaging existing and potential employees.

What about the resources required for reporting?

This is obviously a key consideration. In our last report, we questioned the cost of our total reporting process. Even our stakeholders were asking how much this was costing. For us, because our business is sustainability, our main cost is the salary cost of internal resources. Our own people write our reports. However, against this cost, we offset the very valuable training opportunity this provides. Writing a sustainability report is one of the best training exercises for new consultants that you can provide.

Top tips for SME reporters?

1. Keep it simple.

2. Spend the time understanding what your material issues are and what's really important to the business and the stakeholders. Whittle it down to a few things and focus on those.

3. Tell your story in an authentic way. Storytelling is an important aspect of reporting. Make sure you know how to tell your story.

Perspectives from the three case studies

One of the things that strikes you as you talk to SME business leaders is the measure of their commitment to transparency in their business, both because it seems like the right thing to do, as a way to demonstrate integrity and build trust, but also because there are very clear business benefits ranging from motivation of staff to customer appreciation to access to lower-cost finance.

SMEs do not necessarily give themselves an easy ride. While the 'keep it simple' theme prevails, none of the SME reporters I talked to have approached transparency as a minimalistic tick-box exercise. All have thought deeply about their role as a business and impacts on stakeholders, and all have tried to respond in the most serious way they know how.

Unequivocally, SME reporting was confirmed to bring business benefits in different ways and with regards to different stakeholder groups. None of our SME reporters regret the investment made in reporting, though all confirm that this investment has to be manageable and managed.

SME reporters also have made use of known and leading practice frameworks – the UNGC Ten Principles or the GRI Reporting Framework. This is both to avoid 'reinventing the wheel' by utilising recognised and established tools, and also to position SME reports as best practice, in line with the expectations of large customers who generally use these tools themselves.

Finally, there is no truth to the myth that transparency is a competitive threat. Clearly, reporting must not reveal business secrets that represent a competitive advantage, such as forthcoming innovations, but providing a full, complete and balanced picture of a company's triple bottom line performance does not seem to have harmed these businesses and has actually contributed to ongoing success and sustainable growth.

....

CHAPTER 4

The Roadmap to Transparency for SMEs

IN THIS CHAPTER, WE WILL:

- Introduce our Five M Model for SME Transparency™.

- Explain the options, challenges and different approaches along the way.

- Provide some examples of good SME approaches and best practice.

Having established that transparency is as much of a necessity for long-term business sustainability, resilience and profitability for SMEs, we now start the journey of understanding the way forward and the options available to SMEs. As usual, given the vast diversity of SMEs around the world, one size may not fit all, so this approach should be taken as one possible route of which there may be many others. The real test is in the implementation. Arguably, larger, complex, multi-country and even multi-sector businesses will have a more challenging task at each stage of the roadmap. The advantages that SMEs inherently enjoy make this process rather more straightforward, although still requiring leadership, discipline, application and a willingness to display transparency.

....

FIGURE 5. The Five M Model™ – SME roadmap to transparency

Mission

Materiality

Measure	Manage

Manifest

....

Mission

Every company, large or small, irrespective of location, sector, industry, operating model, state of evolution and any other factor relating to the business, has a social mission alongside its financial mission, which is usually expressed in the financial bottom line of revenues, profit and often growth.

The social mission of the business refers to the contribution a company makes to society in addition to the fact that it makes money. This concept, as far as I know, was first introduced by Christine Arena in her enlightening book *The High Purpose Company* (HarperBusiness, 2006), in which she demonstrated how large businesses achieve stronger results over time when they are driven by a higher social purpose.

Examples of the social purpose, or mission, of business can be found quite frequently these days in corporate communications. I often cite the example of Wal-Mart, whose original business was built on the tag-line 'Always low prices'. This suggests that the reason customers shopped at Wal-Mart was to achieve money savings. This is fine, and attractive, as far as it goes. However, some years ago, Wal-Mart changed its tagline to 'Save Money. Live Better'. See that? Now, the tag-line refers to not only the benefit of financial gain, but also the impact of that financial gain on customers. When you save money on groceries, you have more money to do other things that improve the quality of your life: invest in education, pay medical bills, take a vacation, participate in cultural activities, etc. The new Wal-Mart promise is about a social mission of helping people to improve their lives, not just bolster their bank account. Isn't that more inspiring, not only for Wal-Mart customers but also for the millions of Wal-Mart employees who now feel they are part of something which transcends a simple cash calculation?

[22]

[23]

Other examples might include Campbell Soup's 'Nourishing Lives'[24] (doesn't that sound better than 'making a profit selling soup'?), or Nokia's 'Connecting People'[25] (prefer that to 'selling mobile phones'?). Examples abound.

The first stage, therefore, in embarking on any sort of sustainability or transparency journey is to clearly define and articulate the social contribution that your company makes. You have to answer the question:

What value do you add to society beyond making money?

This value may be improving people's lives in some way or another, empowering communities or developing access to medicine, nutrition, technology, etc. It can be as specific as you wish, but a defining a broader framework of contribution can change your business paradigm and help you realise that there may be additional ways to create shared value that you might not have previously considered. For example, communications technology companies often talk about digital inclusion. This is a form of social mission. By focusing on digital inclusion, rather than selling technology, companies have realised ways to penetrate new markets, especially emerging economies, with targeted innovative products that meet the needs of these markets and enable local communities to develop livelihoods and participate more effectively in the global economy.

As an SME embarking on the sustainability journey, the first stage is to define your social mission.

ACTION PLAN

Take a day out of the business. It won't collapse in one day. You can make the time. Involve your employees. Think deeply about what you add to society. Think about the words that you can use to articulate the higher purpose for your company, that so that it is both inspiring for you and clear to your external stakeholders. Stop the merry-go-round for a day and have this conversation. If you have the funds to bring in an external expert who can help you to facilitate the conversation, this is often a good idea, but if not, just do it with your colleagues. Once you have developed your social mission, think about what this means for your product or service offering. Instead of selling your service, sell your social mission. This might require you to think about a new way of communicating with your employees and customers. Define the directions that this might take.

Materiality

The concept of materiality in sustainability practitioners' jargon simply means the issues which are of greatest importance to your business continuity and success and to your internal and external stakeholders. Typically, a business is advised to engage with a range of stakeholders in order to understand their concerns and aspirations, and examine these in the light of business strategy. Once the key issues for stakeholders are understood in the context of an organisation's business objectives, they can be assessed and prioritised for action. Most businesses today, for example, will hear stakeholders talking about environmental protection or low-carbon economy, or safety, quality and fair conditions for employees. Some businesses will hear very specific issues from stakeholders depending on the business sector, location and current economic climate. For example, companies in the cosmetics sector may hear concerns about testing on animals.

Larger corporations have the resources to engage in broad stakeholder engagement processes, ranging from stakeholder surveys to roundtable discussions with different groups. Larger organisations are often members of trade associations which enable them to engage on industry issues with a view to effecting change at national or global level.

SMEs, however, have fewer resources available and opportunities to engage with stakeholders may be less obvious. On the other hand, SMEs are inherently closer to their customers, employees and suppliers, and are often involved with local community life, because of the more personal nature of smaller businesses. SMEs, therefore, have natural opportunities to engage on matters of importance. What is needed is to add a little structure to this kind of engagement, so that the key issues are presented and understood. In conversations with customers, suppliers, local community partners, etc., SMEs should raise questions in relation to their social mission and the value that stakeholders gain. Each interaction with stakeholders can become an opportunity to find out what stakeholders find important about the SMEs business activities and impacts. SMEs should document these interactions in a structured way, to create a reflection of the collective interests of stakeholders, which can then be prioritised and assessed. By integrating stakeholder engagement into regular business interactions, SMEs can gain valuable insights into how to advance their business in alignment with both strategic objectives and targets and stakeholder expectations. Alternatively, SMEs can use low-cost, minimum-resource ways to ensure they are in tune with their stakeholder views. These may be in the form of customer satisfaction surveys, either online or printed, or through use of social media such as a company blog or Facebook page announcing company news and developments.

ACTION PLAN

List your key stakeholder groups – employees, customers, suppliers, community partners, local municipalities, local environmental organisations, finance providers, etc. Against each one, list what it is they want from your business beyond their financial interaction with you. Employees, for example, may want opportunities to develop and learn new skills. Customers may wish to have outstanding service, better value for money or raise concerns about product safety. Community partners may want more regular volunteers to assist with certain community programmes. Neighbours in the community may wish you to reduce the noise from your production plant or control air pollution. Finance providers may wish for more detailed information about your expansion plans on a timelier basis. Once armed with the list you have created, make a reality check. Conduct an employee survey, or hold an open discussion meeting with employees to hear their views, identify a representative group of customers and ask them about their interaction with your business and what they need or expect from you in the future, etc. Do the same with other stakeholder groups. This process might take a few months. However, the very fact that you raise these issues with stakeholders is a way of building and consolidating trust. Check if your stakeholders are saying what you anticipated. You might have some surprises. Finally, for each stakeholder group, list the top three issues that are priorities for them. Review all the issues and identify the top five which come up most often. These will become the key stakeholder material issues for your business.

Using these issues, make an assessment of their ability to affect your business development and rank them in order of importance. This is your list of material issues which should inform your ongoing business and sustainability strategy.

Measure

There is probably no-one left on Earth who has not heard some variation on the theme of 'what gets measured gets managed'. It's a popular saying for a reason – it's true. Measurement is both a necessary precursor to management and also a check and control for management. We must measure our basic sustainability performance in order to improve our sustainability impacts through proactive management. There are hundreds of sustainability indicators that larger businesses may track on a regular basis. SMEs as individual companies, however, have both limited impacts and limited resources to invest in sophisticated software and technology to make the measurement process easier. However, it need not be so complicated. There is a set of core sustainability indicators that are relevant for any business, small or large, and which do not require masses amount of resource to measure. A list of 25 essential sustainability measures for SMEs is contained in Table 1.

TABLE 1. Twenty-five essential sustainability indicators for SMEs

MEASURE	EXPLANATION
	ENVIRONMENTAL MEASURES
1 Total electricity consumption per year in kwh	If you are drawing electricity from the National Grid, your electricity bills include consumption information. If you are an office-based business, then electricity is most likely to be one of your largest expenses. By tracking your consumption, you can measure the effects of any energy-saving measures you have installed in your business. The simplest ways of conserving energy are to ensure lights and other electrical appliances are switched off when not in use and that mobile phone and other chargers are unplugged when not charging. This includes wise use of air-conditioning facilities and ensuring temperatures are set to save energy, and that employees do not keep windows open when the air-conditioning units are in operation. This may sound like common sense, and it is, but you may be surprised at the savings to be gained by heightening employee awareness of these practices. More advanced solutions might be to replace lighting with energy-efficient fluorescent options, add insulation to offices, use energy-efficient computer hardware technologies, install motion sensors for automatic lighting when needed and many, many more. By measuring your energy consumption, you can identify the beneficial effects of these changes on your overall costs, as well as improving your environmental impacts. Larger SMEs may consider conducting a full energy and lighting audit by a professional expert. In general, the cost of the audit will pay for itself several times over in subsequent savings.

2	Total consumption of gasoline/ diesel fuel for vehicles owned/ leased and operated by the company in litres	All purchases of vehicle fuels include details of quantity purchased. This figure can help you manage your operational efficiency. Fossil-based fuels are becoming more expensive for many businesses, and car travel is a large part of operational expenditure. Fuel consumption can be reduced by having employees travel more by public transport, car-pooling and by teaching employees energy-efficient driving techniques. By measuring fuel consumption, you are not only keeping track of a key cost in your business, you are providing your company with a basis to make decisions to reduce fuel consumption, for another triple bottom line benefit.
3	Total number of km in flights taken for business travel	Whenever anyone in your business flies, note down the amount of km per flight. This is easy to obtain and often provided with your flight information. This figure impacts the total carbon footprint of your business, and while there is a difference between long-haul and short-haul flights in terms of emissions per km, an average can be used. Measuring and tracking flights may provide insights into options to reduce the amount of flying in favour of virtual meeting options and other ways of working.
4	Your carbon footprint (CO_2 emissions)	For the sake of simplicity in an SME business, which does not have complex manufacturing operations, your carbon footprint can be calculated using the consumption of energy (electricity and fuels) and flights. Larger SMEs may make more detailed calculations, for example, to include additional forms of energy such as natural gas, etc., but for most SMEs without a heavy manufacturing element, this calculation is enough to create a baseline from which to measure ongoing performance. As an SME, your carbon footprint is part of another company's supply chain. Sooner or later, your customers will ask you for this data.

5	Total water consumption per year in m^3	If you draw water from the National Water Authorities, your water bills include this information. Water is a cost to any business, and with the increasing severity of climate change impacts, water is becoming scarcer and its cost is likely to increase in the medium to long term. By monitoring your water consumption and taking measures to reduce consumption, such as water-saving devices on taps and half-flush toilets, you are not only saving money now, and more in the future, you are contributing to a global effort to preserve the planet.
6	Waste generation in kg	This is more difficult to measure and requires a system whereby waste is weighed before disposal. If you segregate waste into plastics, paper, electronics and organics (which facilitates the option to recycle different types of waste) you could route all waste to a single point prior to disposal, invest in a weighing scale and record the weight. Remember that whenever you have waste in your business, you have a potential cost saving, so you may well find that this small change to your daily practice could lead to new insights about potential efficiencies.
7	Waste recycled in kg	If you have installed a system to measure waste generation, as above, then measuring the amount of this waste which is routed for recycling should also be manageable. Recycling waste may be an additional source of revenue generation – selling old electronics, or paper waste, for example. Some companies have created very valuable revenues out of the waste streams of other industries. One that springs to mind is ESM Technologies (www.esmingredients.com). This company has built a thriving international business based on the use of

eggshell membranes as an active ingredient in wellness food supplements for humans and animals. Eggshell membranes are the waste stream of other industrial companies. By considering the amount of waste that you recycle, you may just hit on an option to make recycling a revenue stream, as well as an environmental benefit.

WORKPLACE MEASURES

8	Employee satisfaction	Even in a small business, the satisfaction of employees correlates directly to their motivation, loyalty and productivity. Especially in a small business, high productivity and low turnover is mission critical. Large multinational companies need an entire infrastructure, often web-based, in order to measure employee satisfaction through surveys and internal focus groups. In a small business, where there are far fewer employees, employee satisfaction can be ascertained by conducting open-minded face-to-face conversations, which might even be part of an employee performance review process once per year. For SMEs with more than just a few employees, a written survey could be appropriate and this could be done using a free online service such as Survey Monkey, or by engaging an external company to manage the survey process. Ultimately the measure of your employee satisfaction can be an important indicator of your ability to maintain and grow your business.

9	Number of lost time injuries	Most small companies have no formal safety programmes in place and rarely talk to employees about safety, unless the activity requires attention to specific safety procedures by law. However, there are many safety hazards in office-based work, ranging from position of wires and cables, light and air quality in offices, glass doors, stairway safety, potential for slips and falls, electrical appliances and more. Road safety for employees travelling to and from work is also included in safety statistics. Injuries which create loss of working time are a potentially major disruption and a high cost to any SME. Tracking both the number of injury incidents and the number of lost days due to injury (see next indicator) is a way of keeping tabs on the effects of safety practices.
10	Number of lost days due to injury	Each lost day is a cost to your business. Calculating lost days due to injury may provide insights about how to improve your employee safety. However, it is an employer's duty to provide a safe working environment. This indicator can demonstrate how well you provide a safe working environment and embed a culture of safety in your SME business.
11	Total absenteeism	Absenteeism, or employees not showing up for any reason other than approved leave, is another direct cost to business and potential for business disruption. In the case study of Impahla above, we mentioned a very low absenteeism rate versus other local companies, which indicates strong employee commitment. This is a crucial management measure which affects not only cost, but the company's ability to develop and grow.

12	Gender diversity – male/female employees	Gender diversity is on the radar with many large companies these days, and gender balance, where women are recruited, developed and promoted with equal opportunity, is undisputedly a major business advantage, as women are a large talent pool and bring valuable skills and competencies to any workplace. Many large companies look for suppliers which can demonstrate a positive approach to diversity and inclusion, and a gender analysis of your business will be the data they seek.
13	Management gender diversity – male/female management	In larger businesses, where there is a structured work hierarchy, with two or more layers of management, a test of the effectiveness of gender balance programmes is the number of women that make it into the management ranks. Only when there is genuine equal opportunity at leadership level can a business be on the road to sustainability. As women's advancement is a core aspect of economic development in many communities, SMEs that advance women can be seen to be playing an important role in society, as well as creating a talent pool from a broader selection of candidates, making recruitment more effective in current competitive markets and the 'war for talent'. In some cases, because SMEs may not be the first choice for top graduates, a sustainability report may help your image as a potential employer. SMEs which target recruitment of underrepresented groups in the workplace could actually be providing themselves with a smart business recruitment solution as well as contributing to society.

14	Employee turnover	Turnover, especially in SMEs, is a high cost burden and a business continuity risk. SMEs with high levels of employee turnover are not reaching their true potential. This measure demonstrates SME effectiveness in recruiting the right people and providing a working environment in which they can realise their potential and remain with the company for the long term.
15	Total hours of employee training and development	Businesses which invest in their employees' personal and professional development generally receive a positive return in the form of more effective performance and higher retention rates. While most SMEs are not large enough to have formal, intensive training programmes, enabling employees to work on challenging projects, attend conferences and external training courses, or even participate in skills-based community volunteering, can ensure that employees gain skills and experience which add to their employability profiles. An SME which publishes its commitment to employee development may gain in reputation and attraction of good recruits.
16	Number of employees receiving a formal annual porformance review	Another element in a sustainability-enabled business culture is respect for employees and their right to know how their performance is evaluated. A formal performance review is a valuable investment of time and helps to ensure alignment between the company's mission and vision, expected behaviours, its management and its employees.

17	Number of employees disciplined/ dismissed on ethical grounds	Ethical conduct is the bedrock of any business and this is just as relevant for SMEs as it is for larger businesses. Whether or not the SME has published a Code of Ethics, SMEs should ensure employees understand the expectation of them as the company's ambassadors in all internal and external interactions. A measure of the number of disciplinary actions that have been taken to address ethical misconduct in the business is another way of examining the effectiveness of a company's sustainability management and commitment.

CUSTOMER AND SUPPLIER MEASURES

18	Customer satisfaction	Customer satisfaction is one of your greatest assets. Banarra, an Australian based consulting firm profiled above, confirms that they started to report on sustainability with the objective of catching the interest of customers. Developing a mechanism to record customer satisfaction and managing this effectively not only provides you with insights which are important for your business but also demonstrates your commitment to an essential component of your business sustainability.
19	Customer quality: number of justified quality complaints	Both the measures of product quality and safety are indicators of the healthy state of your business processes and are matters of significant importance to your customers. Tracking the number of complaints is the basis for improvement, and transparency in this area is a bold but progressive move for SMEs.
20	Product safety: number of justified complaints	

| 21 | Supplier satisfaction | Suppliers are stakeholders too and may often be critically important for SMEs in maintaining business continuity. In the spirit of engaging with stakeholders, it is important to understand the way suppliers view working with you and how you make it easier for them to provide you with their best service. A short online survey, or a series of phone calls, will enable you to get a view of how your suppliers view you and your commercial relationship. It might even lead to suggestions for greater efficiency or collaboration or possibly to the identification of risks in your supply chain that could affect your business. |
| 22 | Supplier on-time payment days | Arguably, the most important thing you can do for suppliers is pay them on time. Often SME suppliers will be local SMEs themselves, and cash-flow is acutely important. By ensuring your suppliers know they will be paid on time, you are not only safeguarding your own business, you are making a positive contribution to local economic development. |

COMMUNITY MEASURES

| 23 | Cash and in-kind donations to local community causes | As an SME, you probably will not have large amounts of cash to donate to the community. However, you may produce products which have value – for example, a small bakery chain may donate unsold products to a local food bank, or a fashion store may give garments to a charity shop. These products have value. As part of your overall community investment, it makes sense to track the value of all the cash and in-kind donations you make in a given year. This helps you understand the actual cost of your commitment, while publishing your investment, even if it's modest, is another way of building trust and credibility with local communities. As your employees are often members of the very local communities you support, they will also find this motivating. |

24	Number of employees volunteering in the community	This shows how engaged your employees are in your community causes, which align with your business mission. It also demonstrates your employees' motivation to make a contribution to the community and be good citizens. Data show that volunteering enhances motivation, productivity and often skills. Providing opportunities for your employees to volunteer in the community is a positive step for SMEs. In addition, it contributes to strengthening the bond between your business and the local community, in which many of your key stakeholders reside. Recording the number of volunteers (and hours of volunteering) requires a simple system for logging such activity. A file sharing mechanism using online cloud applications such as Google Docs or other formats can be sufficient for the very small business, though larger SMEs may need a more robust software solution.
25	Total hours of community volunteering	Time is money. In the US there is a widely used reference for calculating the value of volunteer time on a national and state basis.[26] In 2011, this was $21.79 per hour. Added to the amount invested in the community for cash and in-kind donations, this can demonstrate quite a significant investment which will be appreciated by your local community.

ACTION PLAN

Review the Top 25 Sustainability Indicators for SMEs and, if you are not measuring any of these currently, select a number of indicators which you feel would be most relevant for you to track. At first, this could be five to ten indicators. It is important to define exactly what you will measure, the measurement methodology and the frequency of measurement. Put these in place and ensure the process is maintained for 12 months. Review performance against these indicators throughout the year and take decisions, if required, to improve performance. In the following year, you can add more indicators.

Manage

Strange as it may seem, sustainability does not manage itself. As with any business activity, or change programme, performance should be managed in line with an overall strategy, objectives, goals and targets. Responsibilities should be assigned to specific individuals and not left vague. In the same way that Banarra in our case study in Chapter 3 decided to manage its internal sustainability reporting project in the same rigorous way as the company manages client projects, so sustainability must be treated as seriously as any other business goal. Your sustainability goals must deliver business benefit for your company, so it is important to focus on areas which have a positive business effect, as well as a social or environmental benefit. In SMEs, people often multi-task and take on more than their immediate roles, and sometimes, more than they can realistically handle. You need to be conscious of this when making your plan and ensure that it is manageable from the outset.

ACTION PLAN

Using the sustainability indicators you have selected to monitor and track, and the material issues you have identified with input from your stakeholders, make a plan covering two years. Decide on the top three to five things that you want to address. Ensure they are aligned with the business needs. Don't take on too much. Good progress in just a couple of areas is better than mediocre progress in several. Include milestones in your action plan that will help you know whether you are on track during the year and not just at the end of the year when it is too late to go back and make changes.

Manifest

This relates to delivering a report about your activities. Sustainability is not sustainable without transparency. Assuming you have decided to produce a sustainability report, you are faced with several options to make this a reality. In Chapter 5, we take you through the paces in the area of developing and promoting your report.

CHAPTER 5

Guidance for Developing a Sustainability Report

IN THIS CHAPTER, WE WILL:

- Pull it all together and provide a roadmap for action to develop a Sustainability Report

- Discuss some of the key aspects that build trust in your report

- Look at some of the SME reports and differences in presentation and scope

Sustainability Reports

Publishing a Sustainability Report is an advanced approach to transparency for any business, not only SMEs, and requires a strategy, policy and sustained practice in order to report in a comprehensive, balanced and mature way. Even with the sometimes limited scope of SME activity, the potential for thorough and even impressive reporting exists. Every SME has a story to tell. A Sustainability Report can be an ideal vehicle for telling that story while delivering other organisational and relationship benefits at the same time.

Most SMEs are challenged to report for many of the reasons addressed in Chapter 2. They have limited resources and limited budget and are managed, in general, without great structure and defined procedures. I submit, however, that limited resources and limited budget is both a myth and a state of mind which can be changed. The real blocker to reporting is that SMEs do not believe that reporting can benefit them. Once they do find reporting appealing, and I hope that Chapter 3 of this book has encouraged this, the question is how to report and not whether or not to report. In the case of SMEs, reporting on a low budget is perfectly feasible. Collecting data against some or all of the Top 25 Indicators mentioned in Chapter 4 will take time and attention, but does not need to cost money. No-one will criticise an SME for publishing a report which is not designed in the fanciest way. In some cases, this could even be problematic. We supported the writing of a first GRI-based report for the Israeli fashion house comme il faut, an SME employing, at the time, around 250 employees. The report design was so creative that feedback suggested that the visuals were of more interest than the report narrative. (View this report at the following link to see what I mean: http://comme-il-faut.com/user_files/english/Agenda/social/CIF_Eng_report.pdf.)

Clearly, SMEs do not need to go this far. Any report is usually better than no report. An aesthetically prepared Word document can do the job just as well. See for example a report we prepared recently for Comverse, Inc., a US based technology company: http://www.comverse.com/data/uploads/Corporate/Comverse%20COP%20FINAL-26-NOV-2012.pdf. This report is not graphically designed but it gets the message across.

Similarly, there are low-cost sources of support and tools available for SMEs when considering reporting. If there is absolutely no budget for reporting, then use of the GRI Let's Report Template could be a step-by-step option to get started. This is available for download free of charge at: https://www.globalreporting.org/resourcelibrary/English-Lets-Report-Template.pdf

I don't like the template option as I find it both constraining and mechanical. I would urge SMEs to go through the process of thinking, not box-ticking. As an SME owner, I can confirm having done this with the small team at Beyond Business Ltd, and gained immeasurably from the insights of my colleagues. I can confirm that it is the thinking, not the writing, which makes a Sustainability Report stand out. Therefore, I offer a simple framework, not a template, for SMEs to get started with their own Sustainability Report. It's called the Ready Steady Go! Model™. It doesn't get much simpler than this!

This probably looks too good to be true: three simple stages for an SME Sustainability Report. Well, it is simple. It will take some thought, planning, considered deliberation and a lot of time, but it's a simple

Ready!

Steady!

Go!

FIGURE 6. The SME sustainability reporting process: The RSG Mode™

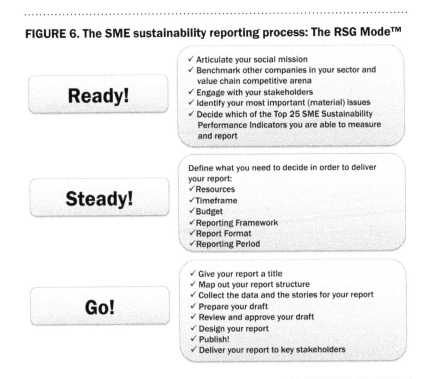

and straightforward process which does not need to be overcomplicated in any way. Let's take a closer look to understand what this means in practice. Figure 6 assumes you have already been on a sustainability journey and know that you have a good sustainability story to tell. It assumes that you have made the decision that you are going to publish a Sustainability Report in some form, and you want to get started!

Ready!

✓ **Articulate your social mission:** by ensuring you articulate your social mission at an early stage, you will be able to create your sustainability story in line with this mission, adding a direction and compelling theme to your report. This will also inform the data and information you need to collect.

✓ **Benchmark other companies in your sector and value chain competitive arena:** get an idea of what other companies, even much larger companies, are doing in the area of sustainability and what they consider to be the most important issues. This can help you think about what is most relevant for you.

✓ **Engage with your stakeholders:** this is not as complicated as it sounds. Given the inherent close relationships with customers, suppliers, local communities and employees that tend to be characteristic of SME operations, extending these relationships to a conversation about sustainability expectations, needs and concerns should not be overly challenging. It's mainly about making the time to do this, and finding the courage to reach out. There are many ways of engaging stakeholders around your report – meetings, phone conversations, email, surveys and roundtable discussions, to name a few. With some effort and determination, you will find that you gain far more from these focused interactions than you had imagined. Identify some key individuals from your core stakeholder groups of employees, customers, suppliers, local community/neighbours and invite them to a discussion about responsible and sustainable business. Conduct the discussion in listen mode, and be open to all suggestions and feedback. If you decide to have a large meeting with 10–20 participants, you should ensure that someone facilitates the discussion so that you can participate in full and listen well.

✓ **Identify your most important (material) issues:** using your core business strategy, social mission, benchmarks and feedback from stakeholders, construct a list of the issues which seem most important to you as a business and to your stakeholders. Prioritise these using a simple scoring system as in the worked example below.

Issue	Importance to the success and profitability of the business score	Importance to stakeholders score	Total score
Product quality	10	10	20
Excellent customer service	10	10	20
Energy efficiency	8	7	15
Employee turnover	8	6	14
Reduced business travel	7	4	11
Dental insurance for employees	2	2	4

In this example, in which six issues (you may have more) are scored, the top three are clearly identified, with the fourth a strong runner-up. I would suggest that three top issues would be enough for most SMEs to focus on in a first sustainability report. You should explain the issues and why they are important (material), providing relevant background and context, describe your response to the issue and performance to date, with a view about your planned performance in the next reporting period.

✓ **Decide which of the Top 25 SME Sustainability Performance Indicators you are able to measure and report:** don't bite off more than you can chew in your first reporting exercise. Decide up front which of the Top 25 Performance Indicators are most relevant for you to measure at this stage, and go with those. You may select five to ten indicators for your first report. You can increase this in a planned way in subsequent reports. Your selection may also be based on what data are easiest for you to collect as well as what seems to be of most interest to your stakeholders.

Steady!

✓ **Resources:** decide who is going to lead the reporting project in your SME, and who needs to support. While this also links to the question of budget, decide whether you need to engage the services of an external consultant. Remember that reporting might look simple enough, but for first-timers it can be quite daunting. If you are prepared to invest in some external support, there are options, ranging from having a sustainability reporting expert review your report once it is in the draft stage and make some suggestions, to engaging a reporting consultant to lead the project and deliver the report content for you. Another creative way for an SME to get help in reporting, at no cost, is to ask for assistance from major customers who already publish their own report and have dedicated experienced staff. Most companies will respond positively to such a request, and this could be a big money-saver while providing you with practical insight.

✓ **Timeframe:** set a deadline for the target publication date, and milestones such as date of first draft, etc. Stick to the deadline! There will be unrelenting pressures from all corners which can delay your reporting project. Don't let them. Make it happen on time, even if it's not perfect.

✓ **Budget:** your budget will need to include external consulting resource as mentioned above, graphic design, if you decide to design your report, and printing costs, if you decide to make a short print run. Decide what your maximum budget is, and review what you can get for your money. Remember that your report has massive marketing value, so treat this cost as an investment.

✓ **Reporting framework:** decide whether you are going to use the GRI Framework for your first report. My view is that GRI represents best practice, and aiming for an Application Level C report is a good start. However, a report that is clearly written, well-structured and provides an authentic view of performance is equally respectable. If you believe you do not have enough information to meet the Application Level C report requirements, or if you simply feel that using the GRI framework is too complex for you at this stage, a non-GRI report can work just as well.

✓ **Reporting format:** decide how you will publish your report. A downloadable PDF is still the most common form of reporting format. More companies are moving to online reports these days, and if you have a good web presence and capability, or if you believe that your stakeholders are mainly those to whom an online report would be preferable, you might put your entire report online (and print a small one- or two-page summary brochure if you need something printed).

✓ **Reporting period**: decide what period you will report. A calendar year? A fiscal year? This will govern the scope of the data and stories you will collect for your report.

Go!

✓ **Give your report a title**: now that you are ready to get moving, stop and think about your report title. I always say that if a report is called 'Sustainability Report' it is missing a fantastic opportunity to engage potential readers from their very first glance at your report. The report title should reflect the key message you want to deliver to your stakeholders. For example, the first Sustainability Report we developed for the SME fashion house comme il faut was called 'Women Who Influence', a title which reflected the company philosophy of empowering women through fashion and making a contribution to society through helping women achieve greater influence. Decide on your title before you decide on your content.

✓ **Map out your report structure**: now you have a title, sketch out the key sections of your report. My best advice is to create a section that covers your material issues and give them prime space. Fit the rest of the content around that. If you have a lot to report, and have been active in many areas of sustainability, you might split the remaining content into some familiar categories: social and environmental; marketplace, workplace, community, environment; or people, planet, profit. There are endless variations. Alternatively, you may run with a series of short sections: product quality, customer service, workplace, employee engagement, community involvement, distribution and logistics, energy efficiency, recycling, and so on, depending on your content. Either way, keep the structure simple.

✓ **Collect the data and the stories for your report:** this is of course the bulk of the work and the most complex part of your report. However, if you have followed the process well so far, you will be very focused on the data you need and the stories that will add substance to your reporting. Try to stay within this plan. Stick to the storyline. Stick to the core data you have decided to collect. Drive it efficiently. It may not be as tough as you think.

✓ **Prepare your draft:** now you can put everything together in draft form. Take care to use a language you are comfortable with. Most companies use the first person to convey a more personal relationship with stakeholders, and generally this works well. Separate paragraphs with relevant short headings make reading easier and help different sections stand out. Once you have your first draft, go over it again and cut out unnecessary words. Aim to reduce your word count by 25% at least. There is always a temptation to write too much. More is not more. More is a headache. Less is refreshing.

✓ **Review and approve your draft:** at this stage, people who have provided content for the report should have the chance to review it and make changes. In addition, you would be well advised to send the draft report, after internal review, to external stakeholders who will give you an honest view and make recommendations to improve clarity or any other aspect. Select people you trust to review your report at this stage, and find a mix between those who know something about sustainability and/or sustainability reporting, and those who do not, so that you get a good range of feedback. After you have digested the feedback, and made relevant modifications, you report is now ready to go to design. Congratulations!

✓ **Design your report:** if you have funds to include professional graphic design, this can make your report more appealing. If you do not, ensure your report is presentable in any document format you choose. Make sure fonts are consistent, headings are the same size throughout, spacing is symmetrical, etc. Ensure photos are clear and will reproduce well in PDF format. (NB: DON'T use stock photos! These are grossly overused and add nothing to your report's attractiveness or appeal. Always use photos of real people, products, places, etc., from your business, and if you do not have any, take some.)

✓ **Publish!:** publishing your report is as easy as posting it to your website. In addition, you should send it to CorporateRegister. com so that it can be hosted there too, giving you more potential for exposure. Additionally, the GRI maintains a Sustainability Disclosure Database[28] that will include your report there too if you advise them of publication. You should prepare a press release to accompany your report publication.[29] There are several free press release options, as well as paid options. If you have a Facebook page, post your report there. Put your report PDF on Slideshare. Tweet about your report (#CSR, #Sustainability).

Google+ your report and blog about it if you have a blog. Send a note to prominent CSR and Sustainability bloggers, and ask if they have an interest in writing about your report. Add a link to your report in the email signature of employees in the company. Get as much free exposure as you can.

✓ **Deliver your report to key stakeholders:** in addition to the above publication activities, you will also want to ensure that key stakeholders know of your report. Send a link to customers, suppliers, community partners, local opinion leaders and of course, employees. In fact, it is worth taking a little more time with employees to ensure they understand the report's significance. Hold discussions about the report, and ask them for feedback. There are lots of opportunities in the months following your report publication to engage your stakeholders in discussion. It should be presented at meetings with customers, suppliers and, in fact, pretty much anywhere you and your employees go. Use it as a marketing tool, a recruitment tool, a conversation point, a source of information and a demonstration of your commitment to responsible business. Proactively invite people to take interest. You have invested significant efforts in producing your report. Make the most of it!

While some SME reporters manage to deliver a very comprehensive first report, there are some who want to get their message out there and do so in a very simple but effective way. You can find any number of examples between the advanced approach of Impahla Clothing and the most minimalist publications. Remember that 80% of something is better than 100% of nothing, so whatever you can manage for your first effort is good. However, the more comprehensive a report you manage to deliver, the greater the potential internal and external benefits. In the meantime, see a couple of interesting examples below.

Minimalist SME Sustainability Reports

Generally, any form of transparency is preferable to no transparency at all. Some SMEs find creative ways to deliver a form of transparency around sustainability information which may not go as far as the GRI-based, comprehensive, data-based report, which tends to be what we look for when we hear the term 'Sustainability Report'. Nonetheless, as a way to develop transparency muscles, and ensure that stakeholders know that sustainability is on the agenda, some SMEs communicate sustainability information in a minimal form.

New Seasons Market, an Oregon-based local supermarket chain which prides itself on locally grown produce and giving back to the community, published a first 'Sustainability Report' in 2012 subtitled 'Growing Sustainably'. It starts with a declaration: 'At New Seasons Market, our values are pretty simple: Offer "Friendliest store in town" service; strengthen our regional food economy; be a progressive, best place to work; and grow thoughtfully and sustainably. We're always striving to improve and we're thrilled to be doing this work with all of you.' While this report is just a few pages, it packs a punch and gets the sustainability message across on key areas of impact such as waste reduction and recycling, community giving and fair workplace. The report can be found at the following link: http://www.newseasonsmarket.com/assets/files/2012-sustainability-report.pdf

Alling Henning Associates Inc. (AHA), a communications, writing and design firm based in Vancouver, WA, US, published a Sustainability Report covering the year 2009. The unusual thing about this report is its format: one long scrolling webpage, interactively and creatively designed. Light on content and data, this report nonetheless showcases some of the positive actions this firm has taken to make their business more sustainable and to support clients in developing sustainability communications. The report serves two purposes: it demonstrates that AHA is walking the talk and it serves an example of work that AHA can produce for clients. The report can be accessed at this link: www.aha-writers.com/sustainability/aha_sustain_rpt10.html. This is a simple way for a small business to get the message through, without expending massive resources.

While AHA has not published another report since, the company's website is regularly updated with news about sustainability initiatives. See: http://www.aha-writers.com/in-the-news

CHAPTER 6

A Few More Words About Transparency

IN THIS CHAPTER, WE WILL:

- Review some points that we have not discussed in detail so far

- Wrap it up

Your website

A website is a company's face to the world, and more than ever in the past, the first point of contact with the company. The SME website is the best platform a small business can use to display its social mission and corporate responsibility profile. A website is available, flexible, accessible and useful. If you do not have a website, then work on that before you work on a Sustainability Report. If you have a website, make sure it includes your approach to sustainability and your newly published report!

Social media

Social media are among the most powerful communications tools that a small business can use, free of charge, to enhance awareness, market presence and build a network. This is not the place for a detailed review of all the social media tools available to SMEs but things like

Facebook, Twitter, LinkedIn, Slideshare, YouTube and others are critical to building your business. You should build your social media identity and presence, using this as another avenue to showcase your CSR and sustainability activities and engage with other professionals in this space. As an SME owner, blogger (my business runs five blogs in three languages) and heavy user of social media, I can unequivocally confirm that my business has not only grown, it has survived, because of social media.

Multimedia options

If you like social media and web platforms, you can enhance your reporting and the delivery of your sustainability messages with short movies which showcase your business, people and performance. There are even a couple of companies that I know of which have delivered their entire Sustainability Reports in video format. This may be stretching the idea a little beyond reasonable expectation, but a short video can be very appealing to many stakeholders and help you gain attention. It's worth investing in one professionally made video in which you present your business and sustainability headlines. I confess that I have not done this yet. But I probably will.

Perfection

At the risk of repetition, a Sustainability Report does not have to be a masterpiece. It has to do the job. It must get your message through, clearly, effectively, authentically. It does not have to be perfect. It does not have to cover all bases. Don't get hung up on getting everything right. Just make your plan and keep it moving.

Gain competitive advantage

So, are you convinced that Sustainability Reporting will help you to gain competitive advantage and perhaps even make more money? Improved internal processes, operational and office efficiencies, measuring performance for better target-setting and decision-making, engaging and building trust with stakeholders, motivating and attracting employees, strengthening your relationship with customers, responding to requests for information, accessing lower-cost finance and managing risk more effectively, are just some of the ways that Sustainability Reporting can help you become more competitive and attractive to large corporations and other customers and consumers, if you are actually engaging in sustainability practices.

Don't believe me?

Try it!

Thank you for reading this short book. I hope you found it useful. Please don't hesitate to contact me at **info@b-yond.biz** with your thoughts and feedback. If this book has helped you with your SME reporting, please do let me know. I would love to share your experiences on my blog!

Links and Resources

The Global Reporting Initiative (GRI): www.globalreporting.org

GRI is a global non-profit multi-stakeholder organisation which acts to increase the level of social and environmental reporting among companies throughout the world. The main way of assimilating this process is the development and dissemination of the GRI Reporting Framework which contains detailed guidelines for reporting on sustainability impacts and provides a consistent structure which thousands of companies around the world now use for sustainability reporting.

The UN Global Compact: www.unglobalcompact.org

Aside from the UN Global Compact's basic Ten Principles framework and explanations about how to use the principles, the UN Global Compact website is a major repository for information and reports relating to responsible business and programmes in place at the UNGC and other UN agencies. The Participant Search feature enables you to see whether your customers, suppliers or competitors are participating in the UNGC and whether they have produced an annual Communication on Progress.

The European Commission CSR and SMEs
http://ec.europa.eu/enterprise/policies/sustainable-business/
corporate-social-responsibility/sme/index_en.htm

This is the website to keep you up to date on what's happening in Europe with regard to SMEs and CSR, and contains some useful resources.

My Business and Human Rights

http://ec.europa.eu/enterprise/policies/sustainable-business/files/
csr-sme/human-rights-sme-guide-final_en.pdf

This is 28-page guide published by the European Commission on human rights for small- and medium-sized enterprises. It covers questions such as why human rights is relevant for SMEs, impact on profitability, human rights and the law, and contains an introduction to six basic steps expected of business-owners/leaders according to the UN Guiding Principles. It is written in plain, everyday language, explains all the professional terms used in this field and makes for very enlightening reading. I recommend this as compulsory reading for all SMEs.

Let's Report Template of the GRI Reporting Framework

https://www.globalreporting.org/resourcelibrary/English-Lets-Report-Template.pdf

A document published by the GRI to assist first-time reporters by providing a fill-in-the-blanks template for a first low transparency (Application Level C) Sustainability Report. While this indeed offers a step-by-step guide to responding to GRI requirements, and may offer some additional insight and structure to help new reporters get started, it should be used with caution. The start point for any Sustainability Report is not a template, but a vision, a story and a set of materially relevant issues. By working through the template, you are likely to address the detail but not the bigger picture. However, for those SMEs reporting for the first time, wanting to make a start in their transparency journey, this template may be a useful tool if used wisely.

The UN Global Compact Operational Guide for Medium-Scale Enterprises

http://www.unglobalcompact.org/docs/news_events/8.1/
Operational_guide_ME.pdf

Although dating back to 2007, this guide provides a step-by-step approach to participating in the responsible business Ten Principle model of the United Nations Global Compact and covers four main areas: Human Rights; Labour Standards; Environment; and Anti-Corruption. The guide maintains that medium-sized enterprises can increase their competitiveness through responsible business actions.

SMEs Set their Sights on Sustainability: Case Studies of SMEs from the UK, US and Canada

http://www.aicpa.org/interestareas/businessindustryandgovernment/
resources/sustainability/downloadabledocuments/sustainability_
case_studies_final%20pdf.pdf

Published in 2011, this interesting guide demonstrates through case studies the different approaches of SMEs to sustainability, providing fascinating insights and key lessons from a range of SMEs in different sectors.

Small, Smart and Sustainable – Experiences of SME Reporting in Global Supply Chain

https://www.globalreporting.org/resourcelibrary/Small-Smart-
Sustainable.pdf

This 2008 GRI research report discusses the added value of reporting for SME suppliers in emerging economies. It aims to provide an answer to the question 'what is the added value of the sustainability reporting process for SME suppliers in emerging economies and their multinational buyers?' by examining and sharing experiences from over a year of the 'Transparency in the Supply Chain' project, a joint project by the GRI and Deutsche Gesellschaft fuer Technische Zusammenarbeit (GTZ) GmbH, which is implementing the PPP-program on behalf of the German Federal Ministry for Economic Development and Cooperation (BMZ). The document shares interesting experiences and insights from the project participants.

Responsible Entrepreneurship – Best Practice Examples from SMEs in Europe
http://ec.europa.eu/enterprise/policies/sustainable-business/files/responsible_entrepreneurship/doc/resp_entrep_en.pdf
This paper, published by the European Commission, is a little dated (2003) but it contains a range of good practice examples from SMEs in Europe which are interesting to read and learn from.
....

Notes

1. http://www.nikebiz.com/crreport/content/workers-and-factories/3-2-1-profile-of-factories.php?cat=profiles (accessed 24 October 2012).

2. http://ec.europa.eu/enterprise/policies/sme/facts-figures-analysis/performance-review/files/supporting-documents/2012/annual-report_en.pdf (accessed 24 October 2012).

3. http://ec.europa.eu/europe2020/europe-2020-in-a-nutshell/eu-tools-for-growth-and-jobs/index_en.htm (accessed 24 October 2012).

4. http://www.apec.org/Press/News-Releases/2012/0803_smemm.aspx (accessed 24 October 2012).

5. http://www.census.gov/econ/smallbus.html# (accessed 24 October 2012).

6. http://ec.europa.eu/enterprise/policies/sme/facts-figures-analysis/sme-definition/index_en.htm (accessed 23 October 2012).

7. http://www.usitc.gov/publications/332/pub4125.pdf (accessed 23 October 2012).

8. http://www.china-briefing.com/news/2011/07/07/china-issues-classification-standards-for-smes.html (accessed 24 October 2012).

9. http://www.unilever.com/sustainable-living/ The Unilever Sustainable Living Plan, launched in 2010, is a ten-year programme focusing on improving Unilever impacts through the entire value chain, including many aspects of consumer behaviour, while enabling Unilever to grow its business.

10. http://www.kingfisher.com/netpositive/index.asp?pageid=1 (accessed 14 January 2013).

NOTES

11. http://hbr.org/2011/01/the-big-idea-creating-shared-value (accessed 14 January 2013).

12. Multinational Enterprise.

13. http://www.kpmg.com/PT/pt/IssuesAndInsights/Documents/corporate-responsibility2011.pdf

14. http://www.mhpm.com/en/csr/20102011csr.aspx

15. www.globalreporting.org. See also Links and Resources section.

16. www.corporateregister.com

17. External verification: in this short book about sustainability reporting, I have deliberately not opened up the verification debate. Around 20–30% of all reports published are verified by an external third party. This serves to add credibility. For SMEs, however, the effort of reporting is mostly significant enough without adding an additional layer of external checking. Rightly or wrongly, I have decided to avoid this debate in this short book, assuming that most SMEs will not seriously consider external verification at an early stage of their reporting.

18. http://sustainabledevelopment.un.org/index.php?page=view&type=1006&menu=1348&nr=771

19. http://www.unglobalcompact.org/docs/news_events/8.1/UNGC_Annual_Review_2010.pdf

20. http://www.unglobalcompact.org/docs/news_events/8.1/UNGC_Annual_Review_2010.pdf

21. www.surveymonkey.com

22. Logo Picture appearing in cracked.com (accessed 8 December 2012).

23. Logo from www.walmart.com

24. http://www.campbellsoupcompany.com/csr/default.aspx (accessed 14 January 2013).

25. http://www.nokia.com/global/about-nokia/about-us/about-us (accessed 14 January 2013).

26. http://www.independentsector.org/volunteer_time

27. The new GRI G4 guidelines to be published in May 2013 may remove Application Levels and make the reporting challenge for SMEs much thought [AQ: tougher?] with a new minimum disclosure threshold. The jury is still out as to whether the new GRI G4 will be good for SMEs, or impossible. This will become clearer in May 2013 when G4 is planned to be launched.

28. http://database.globalreporting.org/ (accessed 14 January 2013).

29. Here is an example of an SME press release for a UNGC Communication on Progress. CSRwire, LLC is an SME that maintains annual reporting to the UN Global Compact: http://www.csrwire.com/press_releases/35040-CSRwire-Releases-Third-Annual-United-Nations-Global-Compact-Communication-on-Progress

For Product Safety Concerns and Information please contact our EU
representative GPSR@taylorandfrancis.com
Taylor & Francis Verlag GmbH, Kaufingerstraße 24, 80331 München, Germany

www.ingramcontent.com/pod-product-compliance
Ingram Content Group UK Ltd.
Pitfield, Milton Keynes, MK11 3LW, UK
UKHW040928180425
457613UK00011B/298